FIRST PIECES FOR
CLASSICAL GUITAR

Compiled and Edited by Mark Phillips

ISBN 978-1-4803-6401-1

HAL•LEONARD®
CORPORATION

7777 W. BLUEMOUND RD. P.O. BOX 13819 MILWAUKEE, WI 53213

In Australia Contact:
Hal Leonard Australia Pty. Ltd.
4 Lentara Court
Cheltenham, Victoria, 3192 Australia
Email: ausadmin@halleonard.com.au

Visit Hal Leonard Online at
www.halleonard.com

Allegretto in A

By Otto Feder

Allegretto

Allegretto in C

By Fernando Sor

Allegro in A Minor

By Dionisio Aguado

Allegro

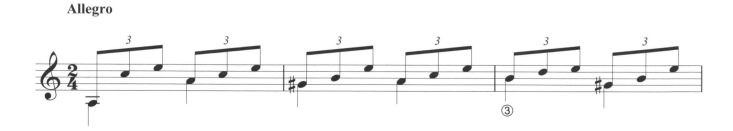

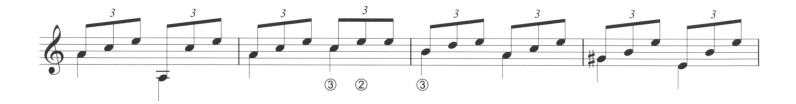

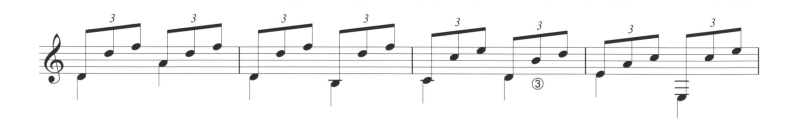

Allegro in A Minor

By Mauro Giuliani

Andantino grazioso in C

By Matteo Carcassi

Andante in A Minor

By Matteo Carcassi

Andante in A Minor

By Otto Feder

Andante

Andante in A Minor

By Fernando Sor

Andante in C

By Matteo Carcassi

Andante

Andante in C

By Mauro Giuliani

Andante in C

By Fernando Sor

Andante in C

By Fernando Sor

Andante in E Minor

By Fernando Sor

Andante

Andante in G

By Johann Kaspar Mertz

Andantino in A Minor

By Ferdinando Carulli

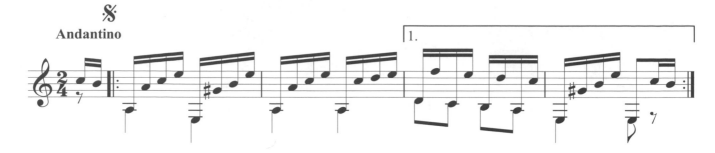

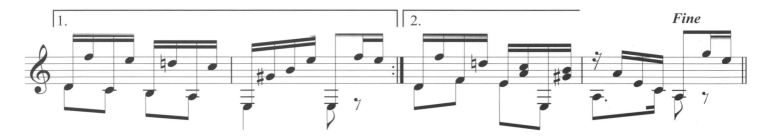

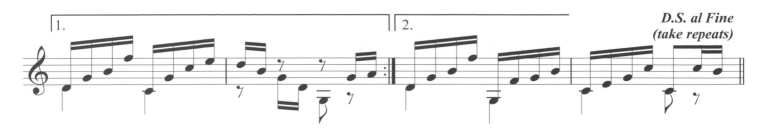

Andantino in A Minor

By Johann Kaspar Mertz

Andantino in C

By Matteo Carcassi

Andantino

Andantino in C

By Fernando Sor

Andantino

Andantino in G

By Ferdinando Carulli

Andantino

Austrian Waltz in C

By Philip Ernst

Bohemian Waltz in C

By Philip Ernst

Bourrée in C

By Graf Bergen

Moderately

Contradance in C

By Ferdinando Carulli

Contradance in G

By Ferdinando Carulli

Moderately

Fine

2nd time, D.C. al Fine
(take repeats)

Ecossaise in A Minor

By Mauro Giuliani

Gigue in C

By Johann Anton Logy

Larghetto in A Minor

By Fernando Sor

Larghetto

Minuet in A Minor

By Johann Anton Logy

Moderately

Romance in A Minor

By François Molino

Moderately slow, in 2

Siciliano in A Minor

By Matteo Carcassi

Study in A Minor

By Dionisio Aguado

Moderately

Study in A Minor

By Dinoisio Aguado

Study in A Minor

By Antonio Cano

Moderately

Study in C

By Anton Diabelli

Moderately

Study in C

By Julio Sagreras

Moderately, in 4

Study in C

By Julio Sagreras

Moderately

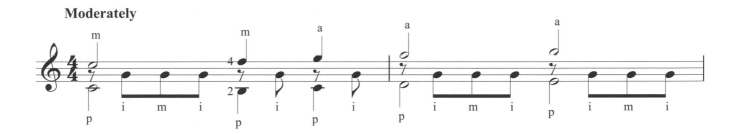

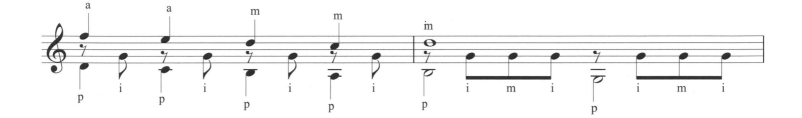

Study in G

By Dionisio Aguado

Moderately

Waltz in C

By Matteo Carcassi

Waltz in C

By Philip Ernst

Moderately

Waltz in E

By Ferdinando Carulli

Waltz in E

By Ferdinand Pelzer

Moderately

Waltz in E Minor

By Ferdinando Carulli

Waltz in G

By Dionisio Aguado

Moderately

Waltz in G

By Matteo Carcassi

Moderately

Waltz in G

By Ferdinando Carulli